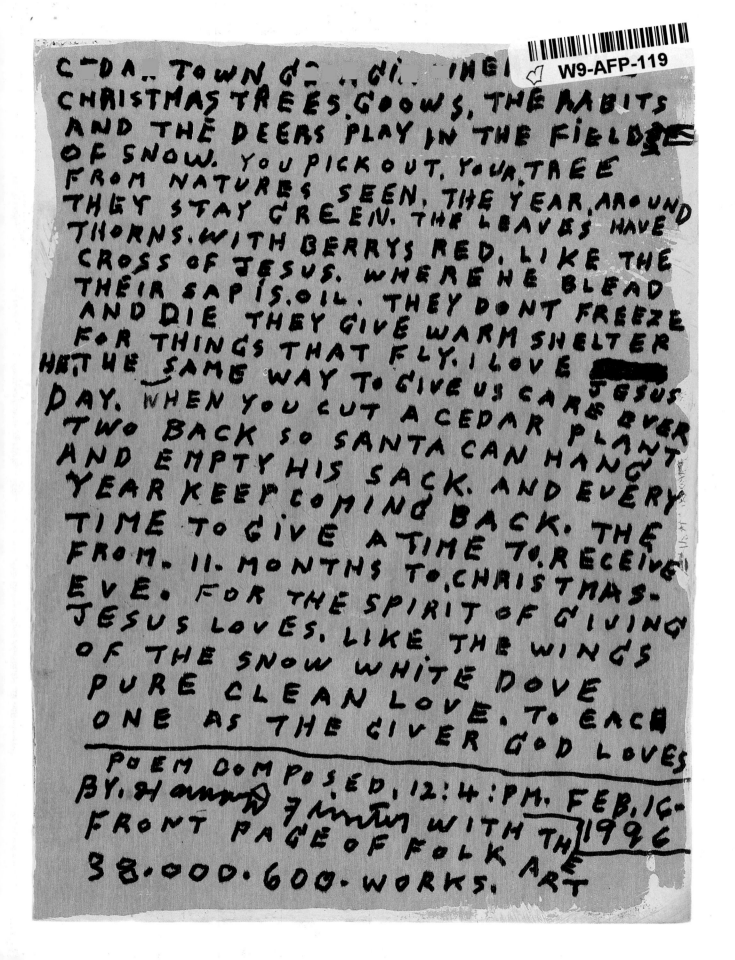

CEDAR TOWN GEORGIA WHERE
CHRISTMAS TREES GROWS, THE RABITS
AND THE DEERS PLAY IN THE FIELDS
OF SNOW. YOU PICK OUT YOUR TREE
FROM NATURES SEEN, THE YEAR AROUND
THEY STAY GREEN. THE LEAVES HAVE
THORNS WITH BERRYS RED. LIKE THE
CROSS OF JESUS. WHERE HE BLEAD
THEIR SAP IS OIL. THEY DONT FREEZE
AND DIE THEY GIVE WARM SHELTER
FOR THINGS THAT FLY. I LOVE JESUS.
HE THE SAME WAY TO GIVE US CARE EVER
DAY. WHEN YOU CUT A CEDAR PLANT
TWO BACK SO SANTA CAN HANG
AND EMPTY HIS SACK. AND EVERY
YEAR KEEP COMING BACK. THE
TIME TO GIVE A TIME TO RECEIVE
FROM. 11. MONTHS TO CHRISTMAS.
EVE. FOR THE SPIRIT OF GIVING
JESUS LOVES. LIKE THE WINGS
OF THE SNOW WHITE DOVE
PURE CLEAN LOVE. TO EACH
ONE AS THE GIVER GOD LOVES.

POEM COMPOSED. 12:4:PM. FEB. 16-
BY. Harmon Finster WITH THE 1996
FRONT PAGE OF FOLK ART
38.000.600.WORKS.

LIBRARY OF CONGRESS CATALOGING-IN-PUBLICATION DATA

MOORE, CLEMENT CLARKE, 1779–1863
    THE NIGHT BEFORE CHRISTMAS/POEM BY CLEMENT C. MOORE; PAINTINGS
BY HOWARD FINSTER.
      P. CM.
   ISBN 1–57036–358–7 (ALK. PAPER)
     1. SANTA CLAUS—JUVENILE POETRY. 2. CHRISTMAS—JUVENILE POETRY.
3. CHILDREN'S POETRY, AMERICAN. I. FINSTER, HOWARD, 1916–   .
II. TITLE.
PS2429.M5N5   1996   96–17725
811'.2—DC20   CIP

PROJECT EDITORS: KEN GEIST, MICHON WISE
ACQUISITIONS EDITOR: KEN GEIST
DESIGNED AND EDITED BY MICHAEL J. WALSH
ARTIST PORTRAIT PHOTOGRAPH BY PHILIN PLASH
PUBLISHED BY TURNER PUBLISHING, INC.
A SUBSIDIARY OF TURNER BROADCASTING SYSTEM, INC.
1050 TECHWOOD DRIVE, N.W.
ATLANTA, GEORGIA 30318

FIRST EDITION
10 9 8 7 6 5 4 3 2 1

THE NIGHT BEFORE CHRISTMAS

CLEMENT C. MOORE

PAINTINGS BY HOWARD FINSTER

TURNER PUBLISHING, INC.

ATLANTA

BY. Howard Finster

AN-25-1996

'TWAS THE NIGHT BEFORE CHRISTMAS,

WHEN ALL THROUGH THE HOUSE

NOT A CREATURE WAS STIRRING,

NOT EVEN A MOUSE;

THE STOCKINGS WERE HUNG

BY THE CHIMNEY WITH CARE,

IN HOPES THAT ST. NICHOLAS

SOON WOULD BE THERE.

THE CHILDREN WERE NESTLED ALL SNUG IN THEIR BEDS, WHILE VISIONS OF SUGARPLUMS DANCED IN THEIR HEADS; AND MAMMA IN HER KERCHIEF, AND I IN MY CAP, HAD JUST SETTLED DOWN FOR A LONG WINTER'S NAP,

WHEN OUT ON THE LAWN

THERE AROSE SUCH A CLATTER,

I SPRANG FROM MY BED

TO SEE WHAT WAS THE MATTER.

AWAY TO THE WINDOW

I FLEW LIKE A FLASH,

TORE OPEN THE SHUTTERS

AND THREW UP THE SASH.

DYING DAILY MY LIFE I GIVE, FOREVERMORE I SHALL LIVE MY WONDERFUL RICHES

GAVE THE LUSTER OF MIDDAY TO OBJECTS BELOW,

WHEN WHAT TO MY

WONDERING EYES

SHOULD APPEAR,

BUT A MINIATURE

SLEIGH, AND EIGHT

TINY REINDEER,

WITH A LITTLE OLD

DRIVER, SO LIVELY

AND QUICK,

I KNEW IN A MOMENT

IT MUST BE ST. NICK.

THE FURTHER YOU PUSH GOD BACK THE WORSE IT WILL GET

MORE RAPID THAN EAGLES

HIS COURSERS THEY CAME,

AND HE WHISTLED, AND SHOUTED,

AND CALLED THEM BY NAME:

"NOW, DASHER! NOW, DANCER!

NOW, PRANCER AND VIXEN!

ON, COMET! ON, CUPID!

ON, DONDER AND BLITZEN!

TO THE TOP OF THE PORCH!

TO THE TOP OF THE WALL!

NOW DASH AWAY!

DASH AWAY!

DASH AWAY ALL!"

TO THE BREAD OF LIFE AND NOT THE BONE WITH PURE WATER HOT DESERT SAND AMONG

THE ANGELS IN GODS GREAT LAND TO LIVE WITH THE SON OF MAN IN

THE BLESSING I HOPE YOU WILL DO THE SAME TO PUT YOUR SOUL IN THE MASTERS HAND

AS DRY LEAVES THAT
BEFORE THE WILD
HURRICANE FLY,
WHEN THEY MEET WITH
AN OBSTACLE,
MOUNT TO THE SKY,
SO UP TO THE HOUSETOP
THE COURSERS
THEY FLEW,
WITH THE SLEIGH FULL
OF TOYS, AND
ST. NICHOLAS, TOO.
AND THEN, IN A
TWINKLING, I HEARD
ON THE ROOF
THE PRANCING AND
PAWING OF EACH
LITTLE HOOF.
AS I DREW IN MY HEAD,
AND WAS TURNING
AROUND,
DOWN THE CHIMNEY
ST. NICHOLAS
CAME WITH A BOUND.

HE WAS DRESSED ALL IN FUR, FROM HIS HEAD TO HIS FOOT, AND HIS CLOTHES WERE ALL TARNISHED WITH ASHES AND SOOT; A BUNDLE OF TOYS HE HAD FLUNG ON HIS BACK, AND HE LOOKED LIKE A PEDDLER JUST OPENING HIS PACK.

His eyes, how they twinkled!

His dimples, how merry!

His cheeks were like roses,

His nose like a cherry!

His droll little mouth

was drawn up like a bow,

and the beard on his chin

was as white as the snow;

the stump of a pipe

he held tight in his teeth,

and the smoke, it encircled

his head like a wreath.

He had a broad face

and a little round belly

that shook, when he laughed,

like a bowl full of jelly.

He was chubby and plump,

a right jolly old elf,

and I laughed when I saw him,

in spite of myself.

A WINK OF HIS EYE

AND A TWIST OF HIS HEAD,

SOON GAVE ME TO KNOW

I HAD NOTHING TO DREAD.

HE SPOKE NOT A WORD,

BUT WENT STRAIGHT TO HIS WORK,

AND FILLED ALL THE STOCKINGS;

THEN TURNED WITH A JERK,

AND LAYING HIS FINGER

ASIDE OF HIS NOSE,

AND GIVING A NOD,

UP THE CHIMNEY HE ROSE.

HE SPRANG TO HIS SLEIGH,

TO HIS TEAM

GAVE A WHISTLE,

AND AWAY THEY ALL FLEW

LIKE THE DOWN

OF A THISTLE.

BUT I HEARD HIM EXCLAIM, ERE HE DROVE OUT OF SIGHT,

"HAPPY CHRISTMAS TO ALL, AND TO ALL A GOOD NIGHT!"

MY WORK IS GOING OUT FROM THE GARDEN LIKE A FLOWING RIVER ON

I AM NEVER ALONE. IT HAS MADE MY HAPPY HOME AND ALL MY SINS ARE FOREVER GONE

THE HOST-FIFTY NINE YEARS HAD PASSED AND GONE WITH THE HOLY GHOST

About Howard Finster

BORN IN DEKALB COUNTY, ALABAMA, in 1916, and raised in Pennville, Georgia, the youngest of thirteen children, Howard Finster experienced his first vision at the age of three. He later concluded it was a sign from God that he was to be anointed a "Man of Visions."

At sixteen, having completed only six years of school, Finster got the call to preach, and ministered for more than thirty years while holding a variety of handyman jobs. Married with five children, he retired from the pulpit in 1965, frustrated that none of his congregation remembered his sermons from one service to the next.

In the early 1960s, Finster, at God's command, began his most important ministry, converting a swampy plot of land around his home in Summerville, Georgia, into what would eventually become known as Paradise Garden. Finster filled the exhibit garden with objects he'd accumulated over the years, unwanted items others threw away. He transformed this castoff material into works of art adorning his outdoor museum. At Paradise Garden, Finster worked to fulfill his vision of man's creations existing side by side with God's creations. So, found-art assemblages, hand-lettered religious signs, displays of human inventions, and other unusual artifacts grew up among the natural environment in a colorful amusement park–like setting.

In 1976, after fifteen years of work in the garden, God revealed Finster's special mission through another vision: a figure appeared to Finster in a smudge of paint on his finger and commanded that he paint sacred art. An unschooled artist who feared he didn't have the ability, Finster initially balked, but soon took up the charge. Amazingly prolific, and often numbering his pieces, Finster has completed several thousand more than the five thousand pieces of art he declares God asked him to create.

Finster's celebrated style includes visual imagery borrowed from many sources, popular, historical, biblical, and personal—a stable of familiar figures from the Bible, famous inventors, politicians, and pop stars frequently appear in his work. Working in the folk-art tradition, Finster puts forth his images in a multitude of media—freestanding sculpture, large cut-outs, found-art constructions, wood, dioramas, easel painting, paintings on rocks, bottles, bicycles, and more.

From the start, Finster inscribed Bible verses and religious messages on his paintings, making each an unforgettable sermon that goes out to the world. Finster's work has been shown in museums and galleries throughout the United States, including New York, Sante Fe, Philadelphia, Atlanta, Los Angeles, the Library of Congress and the Smithsonian Institute in Washington, D. C., and around the world from Australia to the Venice Biennale. He's painted album covers for the rock groups R.E.M. and the Talking Heads (voted album cover of the year by *Rolling Stone* magazine in 1985), appeared on the *Tonight Show*, and been featured in the *Wall Street Journal, Esquire, People,* and *Life* magazines, among other national publications. His eight-foot three-dimensional Coke bottle, commissioned as the signature piece for the Coca-Cola Olympic Salute to Folk Art, traveled the world in an international exhibition commemorating the 1996 Centennial Olympic Games in Atlanta.

In the early 1980s, Finster founded the World's Folk Art Church, using an art grant to buy a church building adjacent to his garden. Here he preaches through his art, with which he fills the chapel, and which continues to inspire.

PARADISE GARDEN

This two-acre museum park, open and free to the public, receives tourists, fans, and devotees from all over the world. Here, Finster displays his innumerable paintings, sculptures, and architecture, each of which carries an individual, inspirational message. For more information, or to make a contribution for the maintenance of Paradise Garden, please contact:

FINSTER FOLK ART, #1 HANKINS DRIVE, SUMMERVILLE, GEORGIA, 30747; 1-800-FINSTER